WITHDRAWN

Read All About
Horses

CLYDESDALES

LYNN M. STONE

The Rourke Corporation, Inc.
Vero Beach, Florida 32964

PHOTO CREDITS:
All photos © Lynn M. Stone

EDITORIAL SERVICES:
Penworthy Learning Systems

Library of Congress Cataloging-in-Publication Data

Stone, Lynn M.
  Clydesdales / Lynn M. Stone.
    p. cm. — (Horses)
  Includes index.
  Summary: Describes the history and physical characteristics of the large work horses known for their long, strong legs and wide, flat feet.
   ISBN 0-86593-511-4
   1. Clydesdale horse—Juvenile literature. [1. Clydesdale horse. 2. Horses.]
I. Title II. Series: Stone, Lynn M. Horses.
SF293.C65S76 1998
636.1'5—dc21
                                       98–25091
                                           CIP
                                           AC

TABLE OF CONTENTS

CLYDESDALES

Clydesdales are big, handsome **draft** (DRAFT), or work, horses. Even a Clydesdale **foal** (FOL), or baby, can look a small person straight in the eye.

Clydesdales have long legs with wide, flat hooves. Clydesdale owners often let their horses' silky, white ankle hair grow bushy above the feet. Owners also **dock** (DOK), or clip, the Clydesdales' tails.

Clydesdales are lively, high-stepping horses, but they're also gentle and willing.

Even at the age of seven weeks, these Clydesdale foals outweigh their young friend by about 120 pounds (55 kilograms) each.

THE FIRST CLYDESDALES

Clydesdales were first raised in Scotland in the area of the River Clyde. In the mid-1700s, farmers there decided they wanted bigger, stronger draft horses. They took their draft horses and mated them to Belgian, Frisian, and Flemish horses.

Development of the Clydesdale gave Scottish farmers a bigger, stronger draft horse.

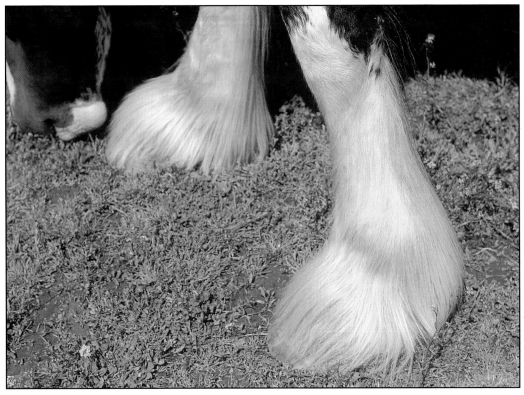

The white, silky hair on the Clydesdale's ankle is called "feathering."

Mixing the **breeds** (BREEDZ), or types, of horses finally resulted in the modern Clydesdale. It was just what the **breeders** (BREE derz) had hoped for—a bigger, more powerful animal.

CLYDESDALE HISTORY

The "new" Scottish horses were first shown as Clydesdales in 1826. By 1850, the Clydesdales were in demand outside of Scotland and England. Clydesdale breeders began shipping Clydes elsewhere.

Clydesdales were popular horses until farm machinery, cars, and trucks pushed draft horses aside. By 1980, Clydesdales were quite rare.

The interest in Clydesdales and other draft breeds has risen in recent years. The number of Clydesdales worldwide is increasing.

Before tractors and trucks, draft horses like these Clydesdales did heavy farm work.

CLYDESDALES IN AMERICA

In the late 1800s, Clydesdales helped to plow the prairies of the United States and Canada. In 1879, breeders in both the U.S. and Canada joined to start a Clydesdale breeders organization. As in other countries, however, Clydesdales began to disappear as motors replaced horsepower.

Today, Clydesdales are probably the best-known draft horses in America. That is largely because they are often seen on television and in live appearances for a major **brewery** (BROO er ee).

White nose, white stockings, and sleek brown coat make a handsome Clydesdale.

THE CLYDESDALE BODY

Each breed of horse has certain features that set it apart from other breeds. The Clydesdale's great size helps set it apart. It stands up to 18 **hands** (HANDZ), or six feet (2 meters) at its shoulders. A full-grown Clydesdale can weigh 2,200 pounds (1,000 kilograms).

Dark brown is typical, but Clydesdales come in a variety of colors.

Grazing is great fun for Clydesdales. Given the chance, they'll graze 18 hours a day!

Compare that to an average riding horse, which weighs about 1,000 pounds (455 kilograms).

Clydesdales have wide muzzles, large nostrils, and large ears. They have a long, arched neck. Clydesdales have very strong feet and legs.

Clydes are usually a shade of brown. They have white trim on legs, belly, and face.

THE CLYDESDALE FOAL

A Clydesdale mother, called a **mare** (MAIR), carries her foal for 11 months. The newborn baby weighs about 150 pounds (68 kilograms) and stands three and a half feet (a little more than one meter) at the shoulders.

A foal's legs look too long for its head and body. But in almost no time the youngster can run and exercise.

A foal grows at first on mother's milk. Soon it adds grass and grain to its diet.

A Clydesdale foal nurses on its mother's milk.
By the age of five months, it will no longer nurse.

GROWING UP A CLYDESDALE

People work closely with the foals. They tame easily, and they like attention.

By the time a male Clydesdale is about two years old, he can be put in a harness to pull. It learns to be driven as part of a pair of Clydesdales. Its partner is an older, experienced horse.

At five or six, a Clydesdale is fully grown. Then it can be part of a team to pull a wagon.

Plenty of attention helps a foal feel comfortable around people. The breed has a gentle nature.

CLYDESDALES AT WORK

Clydesdales were once used to pull heavy carriages, coal wagons, and plows. Horses are rarely needed for work now, so draft horses are used more for show and competition.

Hard at work, a team of Clydesdales pulls a manure spreader across an Illinois pasture.

Life is never all work, even for a draft horse. This young Clydesdale enjoys a spring day's nap.

Many Clydesdale owners, however, still train their horses to pull wagons, sleighs, carriages, or farm machinery. A few large companies use four, five, and even six pairs of Clydesdales in teams. The teams haul brightly painted wagons to advertise the owners' companies.

THE CLYDESDALE'S COUSINS

The Clydesdale's closest cousins are the other heavy draft horse breeds. These horses are built much like the Clydesdale.

Among the breeds used by farmers who developed the Clydesdale were Shires and Belgians.

Shires are the world's largest horses, weighing up to 2,600 pounds (1,180 kilograms). Shires are uncommon in the United States.

Belgians are about the same size as Clydesdales. American Belgians are generally tan with golden manes and tails. Belgians are more common than either Clydesdales or Shires.

Many Belgian horses in Europe are raised for their meat. Fortunately for this Belgian, it's in Colorado.

GLOSSARY

breed (BREED) — a particular group of domestic animals having the same characteristics, such as shape or color

breeder (BREE der) — one who raises animals, such as horses, and lets them reproduce

brewery (BROO er ee) — a place or company where beer is made

dock (DOK) — to shorten or remove

draft (DRAFT) — used for work

foal (FOL) — a horse before the age of one year

hand (HAND) — a four-inch (ten-centimeter) measure of horses' shoulder height

mare (MAIR) — mother horse

Rugged but gentle, Clydesdales have earned the respect of horse people.

INDEX

breeders 11

breeds 7, 12, 20

brewery 11

Canada 11

carriages 18

Clydesdales 5, 6, 8, 11,
    12, 17, 18, 19, 20

England 8

feet 5, 13

foal 5, 14, 17

hooves 5

horses

    Belgian 6, 20

draft 5, 6, 18

Flemish 6

Frisian 6

shire 20

legs 5, 12

mare 14

River Clyde 6

Scotland 6, 8

tails 5

team 17

United States 11, 20

wagons 19

FURTHER READING

Find out more about horses with these helpful books and organizations:
Clutton-Brock, Juliet. *Horse.* Knopf, 1992.
Edwards, Elwyn H. *The Encyclopedia of the Horse.* Dorling Kindersley, Inc., 1994.
Hendricks, Bonnie. *International Encyclopedia of Horse Breeds.* University of
    Oklahoma, 1995.

Clydesdale Breeders of the U.S., 17378 Kelley Road, Pecatonica, IL 61063.